DAVID BYRNE

David Byrne is the Artistic and Executive Director of London's New Diorama Theatre, and a playwright and theatre director. His first play won the Writers' Guild and *List Magazine* Awards for Drama in 2004.

His work includes *Secret Life of Humans* and a new, radical adaptation of George Orwell's *Down and Out in Paris and London*, which both played to sold-out audiences at the Edinburgh Festival Fringe and in London, received four- and five-star reviews in the national press, and transferred Off-Broadway.

David is also a comedy writer, developing both solo projects and joint scripts with writing partner Richard Hurst. *The Party* was optioned by BBC Comedy, after winning their nationwide Laughing Stock contest, and David has had several original pitches commissioned including *Ruthless*, a comedy set in the Royal Opera House and *Stitches*, a series set on Savile Row. His most recent script, *Being Julian*, about WikiLeaks founder Julian Assange living in the Ecuadorian Embassy was performed at the Arcola Theatre, and later optioned for television by Objective Productions with Channel 4.

David is the recipient of several Peter Brook Awards, the Off-West End Award for Best Artistic Director, the Enfant Terribles Prize, and is one of *The Stage*'s 100 most influential people working in theatre.

David Byrne

SECRET LIFE
OF HUMANS

NICK HERN BOOKS

London

www.nickhernbooks.co.uk

A Nick Hern Book

Secret Life of Humans first published in Great Britain in 2018 as a paperback original by Nick Hern Books Limited, The Glasshouse, 49a Goldhawk Road, London W12 8QP

Secret Life of Humans copyright © 2018 David Byrne
Introduction copyright © 2018 David Byrne

David Byrne has asserted his moral right to be identified as the author of this work

Cover image by Guy Sanders and David Monteith-Hodge

Designed and typeset by Nick Hern Books, London
Printed in Great Britain by Mimeo Ltd, Huntingdon, Cambridgeshire PE29 6XX

A CIP catalogue record for this book is available from the British Library

ISBN   978 1 84842 721 1

Woodland
CARBON
www.woodlandcarbon.co.uk
NICK HERN BOOKS
Printed on Carbon Captured paper

Introduction
David Byrne

In a world where major political, economic and ideological divides seem to split whole populations, you can find great optimism in delving back into what shaped and formed us as a species.

Where did we all come from?

What shared history still lives in each of us, just below the surface?

And what, in our ever-present past, can we use to help with our concerns and challenges today?

This play spans several different time periods: Ava and Jamie's lasts a single night, Bruno's story across one lifetime, and the history of humanity across millions of years. Putting them together, we want them to resonate, to give a new perspective on where we've come from, where we are now and where we're going.

Finding Jacob 'Bruno' Bronowski was the key to the development process of this play.

We knew we needed to find a character who had lived through the key events of the twentieth century and who had a connection with our shared history, while always looking forward.

The core of his story in this play is true. Bruno's daughter, Lisa Jardine, made the documentary *My Father, the Bomb and Me*, documenting her own discoveries in her father's locked and alarmed room. In *Secret Life of Humans*, we've imagined the discovery skipped a generation, and the revelations are made over the course of a single night.

It's no surprise then that one of the major inspirations that can be traced through the play is Bronowski's *The Ascent of Man*, both the BBC television series and the accompanying book – without which no coffee table in the seventies and eighties was complete.

The second inspiration is Yuval Noah Harari's *Sapiens: A Brief History of Humankind*, whose grand sweeping narrative warns us that humanity may have veered off-track long ago and that, as a species, we may be heading for disaster.

Whatever their difference, the similar theories in both books on what makes us human convinced us these ideas could live on stage: our ability to communicate together in large groups, our vivid shared imaginations and our capacity to invest in stories and myths.

Everything that makes us human exists in theatre.

And, instead of reading alone about the complex, incredible creatures we are, how much more powerful to come together and sit, side by side, with our fellow humans to look again at ourselves and rediscover ourselves anew.

Throughout the play, there are two major debates that fight it out: 'What does it mean to be human?' And, 'Where are we heading?' Both arguments are strong and compelling, the stakes could not be higher.

For anyone wanting to stage this play in the future, I leave it to you to decide which voice ultimately wins out. I imagine it'll largely be down to the climate at the time, and as to whether audiences are willing to embrace optimism and uncertainty over a more nihilist view of the world.

When staging the original production, we worked to keep audiences aware of echoes of our distant past throughout the story. This was achieved through small moments in the performances and through a beautifully complex sound design, consisting of human voices to keep one of our feet with our ancient ancestors.

Also, as a company, we worked to give the show a fluid style, with no breaks, scene changes or blackouts – one scene melting and transforming into the next, and, once we arrive, never to leave the Bronowski house.

After all, as Bruno said in *The Ascent of Man*, 'a house, a home, is the best place to study our biological uniqueness'.

London, 2018

Secret Life of Humans was first performed at the Pleasance Theatre, Edinburgh, as part of the 2017 Edinburgh Festival Fringe (previews at New Diorama Theatre, London). The production returned to New Diorama on 10 April 2018, ahead of a transfer to 59E59 Theaters, Off-Broadway, on 31 May 2018. The cast, in order of appearance, was as follows:

AVA	Stella Taylor
JAMIE	Andrew Strafford-Baker
JACOB BRONOWSKI	Richard Delaney
RITA BRONOWSKI	Olivia Hirst
GEORGE	Andy McLeod

IN VOICE-OVER

MICHAEL PARKINSON	Himself
CHILD LAUGH	Óscar Varona Liu
VARIOUS VOICE-OVERS	Zakk Hein, Helen Matravers & Kate Bassett
BERTRAND RUSSELL	Himself

Devised by the company

Co-director	David Byrne
Co-director	Kate Stanley
Dramaturg	Kate Bassett
Costume Designer	Ronnie Dorsey
Projection Designer	Zakk Hein
Lighting Designer (*Edinburgh*)	Geoff Hense
Lighting Designer (*London & NYC*)	Cat Webb
Production Assistant	Alex Lui
Aerial Designer	John Maddox
Producing Stage Manager	Helen Matravers
Set Designer	Jen McGinley
Technician	Penny Rischmiller
Assistant Director	Ellie Simpson
Composer & Sound Designer	Yaiza Varona
Executive Producer	Sophie Wallis

Secret Voice of Humans

An album, *Secret Voice of Humans*, heavily inspired by the composition and sound design of the original production of this play is available on iTunes and all major digital stores.

With huge thanks to

Julia Tyrrell, Yuval Harari, Gregor Cubie, Dee McCourt, Mathilda Gregory, Henry Hein, Richard Lakos, Guy Sanders, Charles Diamond, Joel Ormsby, Jo Salkilld, Luís Álvarez, Sofie Mason, James Haddrell, Oli Forsyth, Anthony Alderson, the whole tech team at Pleasance Two, Kate Baiden, Lauren Mooney, Sarah Wilson, Mary Martin, and everyone who runs the pubs in Elham.

Supported by

Secret Life of Humans is a New Diorama Theatre production, co-produced by Greenwich Theatre and Pleasance. The production is supported using public funding by the National Lottery through Arts Council England, The Cockayne Foundation, and PRS for Music Foundation.

SECRET LIFE OF HUMANS

David Byrne

For Sue and Mike,
for unrelentingly giving me places to live and,
without whom, I wouldn't be doing any of this.

Characters

AVA, *early thirties*
BRUNO BRONOWSKI, *late thirties / mid-sixties*
JAMIE BRONOWSKI, *late twenties / early thirties, Bruno's grandson*
RITA BRONOWSKI, *late twenties, Bruno's wife*
GEORGE, *mid-twenties*

There are a few small ensemble roles that can be played within the cast of five. These include:

PARKINSON PRODUCER, *early thirties*
RUNNER, *twenties*
MICHAEL PARKINSON, *mid-fifties, Yorkshire*
HUMAN FIGURES, *two figures, any age*
RADIO, *female, any age*
GERMAN CIVILIAN, *any age*
RADIO PRODUCER, *male, mid-thirties*

Setting

The majority of the action takes place in the Bronowski family home, in present day, over the course of a single night.

This text went to press before the end of rehearsals and so may differ slightly from the play as performed.

Prologue

I

An empty stage. A single chair. House lights still up, AVA *enters holding an old archive box. The play starts in the very room it is being performed in.*

AVA. Where to begin?

I was told a story once, actually, about a theatre group who were doing a show – in a room just like this one. And this one performance only a man and his dog turned up to watch. And not like a guide dog. Just a normal dog. They knew this because, about midway through the show, the man, he got up and left. Went to the toilet. Or to get a refund. Or something. And left just his dog, and only the dog, watching the actors perform.

One by one they all noticed. And they had this dilemma on their hands. Do they keep performing, just for the dog? Or do they stop? They carried on.

So, before we start, I just want to check there are only humans here tonight? Good.

Perfect. That means we're alone. Because tonight we're going to be talking about ourselves. About the complicated creatures we humans are.

We no longer see ourselves as animals. Even though we're covered in the pencil markings of our past. As Darwin said: our bodies each bear the indelible stamp of our lowly origins.

Here's a simple one – stretch out your arm and put your thumb on your little finger. Some of you will see a protruding tendon on your wrist. There's mine – it's quite pronounced. It's useless now. It's a tendon found in primates who use their forearms for walking. Those distant ancestors, they're still here with us.

That's the extent of the audience participation. You can relax…

Slowly the houselights begin to fade.

…Like when you're falling asleep, and you're slowly drifting off, down into the dark, and you jump. Because deep in the well of our memories there are still faint, underwater echoes of when we slept in the trees, holding on tight, afraid to fall.

These are vestigial traits. From the Latin 'vestigia', meaning 'footprints'.

In our minds we are these complex, rich, intellectual beings, full of nuance and philosophy, contradiction and politics, of science and art, of love and sadness. We have gone from animals, to believing we alone were created in the image of gods. And now, finally, to where we are today, all-powerful gods ourselves. Sitting in this lecture theatre, talking and listening.

What I'm about to tell you, it's not strictly part of your course. Some of you will be aware that this is my final lecture. What I want to tell you, it starts now, some of it happened just a fortnight ago. And some of it, it goes back thousands of years. Millions actually. And it's about what makes us human. Of how we've progressed, but we've not changed. How our destiny as a species – in the same way a fruit holds a stone, its future, at its core – has been inside each one of us from the very beginning. About how this, our body, our animal body, is still layered with the footprints of those primitive ancestors. It's still weak, analogue, vulnerable and lonely. Often completely unfit for purpose. This – This is Jamie.

JAMIE *enters. Thirties, smart enough clothes. He is struggling to get into a supermarket salad bowl. He sits on the chair, at home, two weeks ago.* AVA *steps through space and time, to join him.*

JAMIE. Hi.

AVA. Jamie, can you tell us what you're struggling with?

JAMIE. I'm trying to get into this Big Salad.

AVA. Fascinating. 'The human hunter struggles with the Big Salad.' I'm not going to do the voice. 'His blunted claws unable to pierce the seal. He resorts to using his jaw to break through the plastic film. And he's in. Success. Although –

JAMIE *pulls out a small, sealed, plastic dressing sachet.*

JAMIE. Fuck.

AVA. 'Ah – the dressing sachet – celebration is short-lived.' Why are you eating a Big Salad, Jamie?

JAMIE. I'm hungry.

AVA. A basic human need.

JAMIE. And I'm meeting someone tonight, for a first date – and if I don't eat something first I tend to order too much food. And that's not attractive. Apparently.

AVA. Procreation. Vanity. Bad table manners. All human traits. Not exclusively human. This is Jamie just two weeks ago. What he doesn't realise is his date actually is with me. But first we need to go further back into the past.

1974. The Michael Parkinson show television studio. PARKINSON PRODUCER, RUNNER *and* BRUNO *enter in a burst of activity.*

PARKINSON PRODUCER. Just this way.

AVA. – this is Dr Jacob Bronowski.

BRUNO. Please. Call me, Bruno. Everybody does.

AVA. You're looking very smart, Bruno. Nice to see somebody has made the effort. That's a little unfair; Bruno is actually in the 1970s, where everyone tended to dress a little smarter. Bruno is about to be interviewed by Michael Parkinson. Can you tell us why?

BRUNO. The BBC are broadcasting my thirteen-part television series *The Ascent of Man*. Showing our progression from our primitive ancestors to the masters of science and technology and art that we are today. Have you been watching?

AVA. I've seen all of it.

BRUNO. I am particularly proud of the final episode, filmed in my own home –

AVA. Yeah. I think it's really… entertaining.

BRUNO. Everyone's a critic!

AVA. Come on! You can't really believe what you say in your series though – that we, humans, have moved forward in a straight, unbroken line of progress?

BRUNO. Of course I believe it. More every day. We humans are –

AVA. How can you – of all people, Bruno –

They are interrupted by PARKISON PRODUCER. *The stage is prepared.*

PARKINSON PRODUCER. Dr Bronowski – Bruno – we're ready for you now.

BRUNO. Sorry, I must go. Later?

PARKINSON PRODUCER. Recording in five. Four…

MICHAEL PARKINSON *enters, sits in his interview chair, opposite* BRUNO, *and the television recording begins. We skip through the interview as* AVA *watches.*

PARKINSON (*voice-over*). Do you find, Dr Bronowski, that people are frightened of talking to you in the sense that they're a bit overawed by your reputation and your presence?

AVA. What Bruno doesn't realise is that this will be his very last television interview.

BRUNO. The journey of human history is that of a great escape. The escape from poverty, the escape from early death, the escape from famine. Look where we are now. Sitting here with the lights and cameras broadcasting us all over the world. All this, from living in trees. Thanks to the enlightenment, the Industrial Revolution, germ theory, I will live twice as long as my grandfathers. Our lives would be unrecognisable to them. And my life has been so happy. Getting to regularly talk on television with all of you. Yes, I have suffered many private conflicts of loyalty, but I have never had any uncertainty about the meaning of the word 'good', the word 'true', the word 'beautiful'. I have an enormous pride in being a human being. And being alive in the twentieth century. In thirty years from now, who knows, I may be dead. And that makes me terribly sad –

AVA. The moment the cameras stop rolling, Bruno came off stage, collapsed and, soon after, he died.

The studio is cleared. The PARKINSON PRODUCER *hands* AVA *a VHS cassette.* JAMIE *pulls the same VHS out of his box. It plays.*

PARKINSON (*voice-over*). I'm often asked which is my favourite interview. One such occurred just over two years ago when I interviewed a remarkable man, Mr Jacob Bronowski. Sadly, eighteen months ago, Dr Bronowski died. I believe it to be the testament to a rare human being. I shall forever remember this meeting.

BRUNO *is left alone in the empty studio, at the end of his life.*

BRUNO. – terribly sad not because anyone will miss me. But because I will miss them. All the people I shall never meet. And so many more marvellous things will be known. Should you listen to me? A television scientist? Well, yes. It's been such a gift to communicate with you all. And you should be pleased that there are people who have led happy and complete lives. Who can speak from a full heart, and a full mind, all in the same breath.

The video of PARKINSON *dissolves into white-noise static and new footage breaks through underneath. We hear echoes of* PARKINSON *talking about* The Ascent of Man. *Now* BRUNO *is presenting an episode, in the prime of his career.*

(*Voice-over.*) Are the earliest known set of – (*Rewind.*) Are the earliest known set of – (*Rewind.*) Here at Laetoli, in Tanzania, captured in hardened volcanic dust, are the earliest known set of human footprints. Two people, biologically no different from you or I, walking together.

Two HUMAN FIGURES *emerge walking high up on the back wall of the theatre, the audience sees them as if they were looking down on them from above.*

Their footprints are in no way hurried. They walk, side by side, their prints so close together that they must have been holding hands. As they walk, a smaller pair of feet, the footprints of a child, run freely around them.

And then, with no warning, something happens. At the exact same moment something causes them to freeze. And turn. And look.

The HUMAN FIGURES *stop, turn and look, making direct eye contact with the audience.*

AVA. The person next to you, in front of you, you and I, we are all related, and they are our great-great-grandparents. We watch them now from the perspective of gods, at the furthest point humanity has walked down the path they started on. Could it have been any different? Could we have taken a different path?

BRUNO. After the pause, they continue. Walking together until, again, they stop, and look.

The HUMAN FIGURES *stop for a second time.*

It fills me with wonder. What are they looking at? What made them stop? And where, where are they heading?

BRUNO *exits. The* HUMAN FIGURES *continue on their journey and, in the present,* JAMIE*'s mobile phone rings. He answers it.*

1.

II

A busy restaurant

JAMIE (*on his phone*). I'm so sorry, I got caught up watching
    something and – I'm here now. I'm coming in. Hello. Wow,
    it's full. Are you – I'll wave. Now like ten people are waving
    back. Can you see me? Why don't you just come over to me
    and say –

AVA makes her way over to him across the busy room.

AVA. Hi.

JAMIE. Hi. Hello.

AVA. Hi.

JAMIE. This is kind of weird, isn't it?

AVA. A bit.

JAMIE. Amazing though. No need for family or friends or
    anyone to set you up. Swipe, swipe, swipe. And here we are.

They have found their way to their table.

AVA. Do you do this a lot?

JAMIE. No.

AVA. It's great. Gives you just what you need. Nothing more,
    nothing less.

JAMIE. It's my first time, actually.

AVA. Does that mean this is going to be a disaster?

JAMIE. Let's find out.

AVA. Want to order some wine?

JAMIE. I'm trying to cut down. So just water for me, I'm afraid.

AVA. Don't be afraid!

JAMIE. What? Oh, right. Ha.

We snap-cut to later in the evening. The table now covered in wine bottles.

That was lovely.

AVA. Yes. Great taste of –

JAMIE. Alcohol?

AVA. Yes.

We cut to later in the evening, more wine bottles and plates cover their table.

JAMIE. So... um – Brexit?

AVA. I don't want to talk about Brexit.

JAMIE. Great.

Another cut, we're now very late in the evening.

But, yeah, of course, I wanted to study philosophy, but it's not really that practical. You know? Right. I'm going to the bathroom. Wow, I'm more drunk than I thought.

AVA. It's that way.

JAMIE *exits to the bathroom.* AVA *sits alone, composure dropping, suddenly more vulnerable.*

After a minute, JAMIE *returns and* AVA *snaps out of her thoughts. We cut to the plates being cleared.*

JAMIE. Mine? My last name is Bronowski. Bit of a mouthful.

AVA. Bronowski? Like the TV presenter – do you remember him?

JAMIE. Yes. He was – he was my grandfather. I'm surprised you've heard of him. He died forty years ago. How old did you say you were...?

AVA. Put your phone away! It's my area of specialism. Part of it anyway.

JAMIE. It's fate!

AVA. I'm not a big fan of fate. Inevitably, yes. Fate? Not sure.

JAMIE. So you've seen his stuff?

AVA. Yeah, of course. *The Ascent of Man* was a big, landmark series – he was like the first David Attenborough, wasn't he? Obviously, it was pretty lightweight and –

JAMIE. Lightweight?

AVA. His view of the world is a little simplistic. For me. But he was groundbreaking. For the time.

JAMIE. He was – is – incredibly respected.

AVA. Sorry, of course.

JAMIE. I'm incredibly proud to be his grandson.

AVA. You can't have known him.

JAMIE. I heard so much about him growing up. He was an amazing man. All of his TV stuff, which I watched as a kid. I was watching some earlier. It's why I was late.

AVA. Tell me something about him I wouldn't know.

JAMIE. In his house, he had this locked room. Fitted with a silent alarm. Growing up, my dad and his sisters, even my grandmother, weren't allowed inside.

AVA. What did he keep in there?

JAMIE. I don't know.

AVA. Your dad must have told you.

JAMIE. He died when I was much younger, actually.

AVA. And what about your mother?

JAMIE. She's why I'm in town. She died a few weeks ago.

AVA. Oh.

JAMIE. So I'm here. Sorting out the house. And at a loose end.

The final cut of the night. JAMIE *and* AVA *are very close.*

So what made you choose me? It was the hair, right?

AVA. In all honesty? I'm having a bad time and I thought 'I want to do something totally out of character.'

JAMIE. You mean socialising to you is out of character?

AVA. These days? Totally. And I was looking through and I saw you. And I thought –

JAMIE. 'God, he's fit.'

AVA. – Yes. Actually. And it's been a long time since I've thought about anyone like that. And then six hours later here we are...

AVA kisses JAMIE. They are interrupted by their table being cleared. They are out on the street.

JAMIE. I would normally invite you back to mine...

AVA. Oh right. I understand.

JAMIE. No. My mum's house. It'd be a bit weird. I didn't want you to be offended –

AVA. I'm not offended. This was fun.

JAMIE. Good.

AVA. Okay.

JAMIE. Great.

AVA. Wonderful.

JAMIE. Brilliant.

And, with an instant cut, we're at...

The Bronowski house. The main hallway

JAMIE. So, this is my mother's house.

AVA. It's nice.

JAMIE. Where do you want to –

AVA. A bedroom?

JAMIE. There's my childhood bedroom.

AVA. Fine.

JAMIE. With a single bed.

AVA. Or –

JAMIE. There's my mother's bedroom. Or my grandmother's.

AVA. What a choice.

JAMIE. Or we could stop?

AVA. We'll make do.

JAMIE. Give me just a moment then. Don't go anywhere.

> JAMIE *heads out of the room, leaving* AVA *alone. She sees the hallway and large bookshelves for the first time. After a while, she shouts.*

AVA. You grew up here?

JAMIE (*from upstairs*). Yeah, the house has been in my family for years. It was my dad's. And his parents'. My grandfather even filmed one of his documentary episodes here.

> *From behind a large bookshelf, an echo of* BRUNO *appears, he is presenting the last episode of* The Ascent of Man, *filmed in this very room years ago.* AVA *reads one of* BRUNO*'s books, perhaps she's seeing him or maybe she's just imagining what* BRUNO *must have been like.*

BRUNO. Everything has taught me that man's life, a man's home, is the proper place to study our biological uniqueness. It is where man can truly be him or herself. It is where our children, the future, are brought up and moulded. And, yes, it is where all our secrets are kept.

As BRUNO *vanishes behind another bookshelf,* JAMIE *re-enters.*

JAMIE. Hi.

AVA. Hi.

AVA *and* JAMIE *vanish upstairs.*

III

The Bronowski house. A large bedroom

Around 2 a.m., some time has passed. JAMIE *is sitting on the bed and* AVA *is putting her clothes back on. Post-coital awkwardness in the air.*

AVA. We didn't even turn the light off.

JAMIE. Sorry about that.

AVA. I'm sobering up a bit now. My brain's starting to work again. Josh –

JAMIE. Jamie.

AVA. Jamie! Thank you for everything. I probably should be –

JAMIE. Stay. If you want. I'm not kicking you out. I'd like you to stay. Plus it's, like, two in the morning.

AVA. Thank you but I'm not sure I'd get much sleep with the light on!

JAMIE. Promise not to laugh? I've always been a bit afraid of the dark. Not like totally. When I was younger, my mum would always – sorry.

JAMIE*'s speech trails off. There is an awkward silence.*

AVA. Well, it was great to meet you.

JAMIE. Don't go.

IV

AVA *sits on the end of the bed.*

AVA. I really should be – Do you know why you're afraid of
the dark? Why we're all afraid of the dark? Humans, we're
ill-prepared for the world around us. Our soft, vulnerable
skin, unsophisticated sense of smell, our slow run, makes us
easy prey. When night comes, the only way we used to
survive was by gathering together, retreating to safety.

JAMIE. This house used to be so full of people. It's nice not
being alone.

*Slowly the room has been getting darker. The rain outside is
now more present and, in the dark, sounds like it's falling
heavily on foliage in the darkness.*

AVA. We'd look out, wondering what's there, staring back at us,
wanting to do us harm. And it wasn't this tamed darkness.
The dark I'm talking about was proper country dark.

JAMIE. You talk as if you were there.

AVA. I was there. And you were there.

JAMIE. I think I'd remember if I was there.

AVA. Inside all of us, somewhere between our memory and our
imagination, our bodies remember every detail of what that
was like.

AVA *picks up a book next to her on the bed. One of* BRUNO*'s.*

'In the darkest – '

We see BRUNO, *filming on location, deep underground.
His voice echoing off the stone walls.*

BRUNO. In the darkest caves, we find a record of what
dominated the mind of early man.

Why did we do this? Create markings and drawings in places
so dark and hidden?

Here we see expressed for the very first time the power of the
human imagination. In these paintings we made ourselves
familiar with the deadly dangers we know we must face.

When suddenly light flashes upon them – we see the bison as if it were charging at us, we see the running deer, the turning boar. In that moment our imaginations brought our greatest fears to life. And our spear arm flexed, preparing us for the emotions, the fear, the rush, we knew we must control to survive.

Here in the dark is where we first imagined our potential. Seeing, not with our eyes, but through the telescope of the imagination. In the way that –

BRUNO *fades away, and we're back in the bedroom.*
JAMIE *has fallen asleep.*

AVA. – only humans can. It's easy to patronise our ancestors and their cave art. But here we are, tens of thousands of years later, sitting together in the dark, doing the exact same thing.

None of this is real. He's not really asleep. But it's no less real than the value of the money in your pocket. Or the laws we decide to follow. Or the borders of countries we've drawn on maps. Or even human rights. All only real because we have decided to believe in them.

Look at words, for example. What are they really? In essence? They're just lines and circles and shapes. Nothing more. But once we're told what they mean, we'll see that imagined meaning for the rest of our lives. You can never go back to seeing them as just lines and shapes ever again.

We live amongst the threads of a million shared myths. They're unbreakable and our minds are so strong: they're the dreams we can never wake up from.

And it makes me think. What else have we invented? That's so much a part of us that we don't remember now that it isn't real? If, like me, you hadn't ever been told what love was, would you have ever felt it?

JAMIE *jumps in his sleep. Suddenly awake.*

JAMIE. Sorry, I fell asleep.

AVA. I'm sure my students do it all the time.

JAMIE. I'd love to come and see you give a lecture.

AVA. You'll have to be quick.

JAMIE. Why?

AVA. Don't worry.

JAMIE. Can I ask what you're hoping for?

AVA. Hoping for?

JAMIE. From this.

AVA. Oh. Just this.

JAMIE. I've had a really good time.

AVA. I got to see your amazing house. Was your grandfather's room here?

JAMIE. What do you mean?

AVA. Earlier you said your grandfather had a locked room, with an alarm –

JAMIE. That nobody was allowed inside. Yes.

AVA. Right.

JAMIE. Are you sure you want to go?

AVA. I think so – Can I see it? The locked room.

JAMIE. Now? It's –

AVA. Yeah. It's got me curious. If not, it's fine. I'll call a –

JAMIE. Yeah, if you want to, of course… It's downstairs.

2.

V

The Bronowski house. Outside Bruno's locked room

As we travel through the house, the ghost of RITA *walks. She is wearing her black mourning dress.*

RITA. Since my husband Bruno died, I've been wondering how long I should leave it before going through his locked room. Without being too disrespectful. His funeral was around one hour ago. I think that's probably long enough.

RITA *enters the locked room, a small space, with crammed shelves on each side. Picking up a few photographs.*

Why did you do this, Bruno? Hide your things away somewhere so cramped, and dark?

The first time we met, Bruno was modelling for me. Posing completely naked, while I drew him. He wasn't a natural model and was bored stiff almost immediately. I threw him a copy of Blake to read. I didn't think it would interest this mathematician much, but it was the only thing I had to hand. I suppose I can't blame him for getting restless, I did string the sitting out for as long as I possibly could.

If I close my eyes even now, there he is. In every detail.

As RITA *has closed her eyes,* BRUNO *has appeared in the doorway, conjured from her memory.*

And I was wrong. And surprised. That session created two lifelong passions. Him to Blake. And me –

BRUNO. You're in my room then?

RITA. – to him.

RITA *talks to* BRUNO, *although they never make eye contact. She is remembering him.*

I've come to get some of your film reels. It was your funeral today. I wanted to hear your voice.

BRUNO. My funeral? Good turn-out?

RITA. You'd have been very happy. I'm hoarse from talking. I didn't even get any of the vol-au-vents.

BRUNO. I hate vol-au-vents.

RITA. I know, but it was your funeral. I thought chances of you eating any were pretty low.

BRUNO. Good point. That photograph you're holding is one of the most remarkable images ever caught on camera.

RITA. I know. I'm not your television audience. I was the one who first showed you it.

BRUNO. Were you?

RITA. The first human ever to be captured in a photograph. / 1838.

BRUNO. / 1839.

RITA. 1838.

BRUNO. I stand fully corrected.

RITA. There he is. Look at him. Standing, all alone.

As BRUNO *speaks, we hear the sounds from the street surround them in the room.*

BRUNO. He's far from alone. The photograph was taken over seven minutes. The busy crowds racing through the Paris street, they're an invisible blur, lost to time. But this boy, in his cap, stopping at the pump, stood still long enough to make history.

RITA. Bruno, what am I going to find in this room?

BRUNO. It shows that even if we, as individuals, were to stand still, progress would still race all around us. Whether we're ready for it or not. Rita?

RITA. And what's this? This newspaper clipping. He's grieving, isn't he?

BRUNO. Yes.

RITA. I know how he feels. He reminds me of someone.
Come on, Rita. Who is he? Bruno? Why do you have this?

BRUNO. He's – I'm afraid, he's just the beginning.

BRUNO leaves and RITA is alone, sitting in silence.

RITA. Bruno, I miss you so much.

RITA returns to addressing the audience.

And I sat, alone, in his company, too exhausted to move,
until it got dark. I live almost forty more years.

*As RITA leaves, the room returns to the present evening.
Empty and still for a moment, then AVA and JAMIE enter.*

AVA. This is it?

JAMIE. This is it. I think it's just all his notes, old scripts,
television awards. Nothing exciting.

AVA. Then why lock and alarm the room? May I?

JAMIE. Go ahead.

*AVA starts looking through the contents of the shelves,
passing things to JAMIE.*

AVA. Old copies of books – there's a – Is this a charcoal
drawing of your grandfather? Naked?

JAMIE. Yeah. Wow. I think it is. Impressive.

AVA. There really is no resemblance. Old TV scripts, with
handwritten annotations. 'The Ascent of Man' –

*On the other side of the shelves, BRUNO picks up the same
script as AVA puts it back down. BRUNO is rehearsing
lines, making amendments as he goes.*

BRUNO. ' – is always teetering in the balance. As we travel…
as we journey from advancement to advancement.'

AVA. Some photographs of him, clothed. Photographs, more
photographs, old passports. Who is Celia Flatto?

JAMIE. That would be my Polish great-grandmother.

BRUNO. 'Humans have spread so fast all over the world from one single point. Curiosity and an imagined better life made us the planet's most intrepid travellers.'

BRUNO *returns the script to another shelf and exits.*

JAMIE. My whole family is here.

AVA. These boxes are sealed.

JAMIE. Why don't we go back to back to bed...?

AVA. Suddenly, I'm not feeling all that sleepy. I probably will in a bit. Don't look so serious.

JAMIE. Just with everything that's been going on, it's a bit overwhelming to be reminded of them all.

AVA. 1943. 1944. All this is well before his television work. Before anything I know about him. Do you have any coffee in?

JAMIE. I'll put the kettle on. Coffee isn't going to make you any more sleepy though, is it?

AVA. I'm strange like that.

VI

AVA *waits until* JAMIE *has left and, after a moment of hesitation, breaks the seal on one of the closed archive boxes. She pulls out a single letter and starts reading.*

GEORGE. Dr Bronowski, I am a recent mathematics graduate now working with Operations Research for His Majesty's Government, I have been tasked with finding some fellow mathematicians for a matter that I can only discuss face to face. If you were interested and I were to travel to Hull this week, might it be possible to secure a place to meet, where we wouldn't be disturbed?

BRUNO. Dear George, let us meet in the one place at the University of Hull we are guaranteed not to be disturbed by any students: the library.

BRUNO's small room transforms into a large library, bathed with daylight. BRUNO is putting books back on the shelves. AVA remains reading from the small archive box.

University of Hull Library. 1943

GEORGE. Dr Bronowski?

BRUNO is holding a pile of books, that he is carefully returning to the library shelves.

BRUNO. George. Please call me Bruno. Everybody does.

GEORGE. Thank you for meeting me. I've heard so much about you.

BRUNO. Have I been spied on?

GEORGE. Ha. What? Spied on? No. Not by me, anyway.

BRUNO. Evasive. I like it.

GEORGE. You read mathematics at Cambridge –

BRUNO. Guilty as charged.

GEORGE. – the best mathematician in your year – senior wrangler. That's incredibly formidable.

BRUNO. You seem to know a huge amount about me. And I know nothing about you.

GEORGE. There's nothing to tell. May I ask –

BRUNO. Yes?

GEORGE. – why have you ended up as a lecturer here? Why aren't you teaching at your old college?

BRUNO. They did not want me. Or, well, an immigrant like me. Act normal, there's someone coming. Morning. Hello.

We hear a member of library staff passing by. BRUNO conceals the books he's holding and stops shelving.

GEORGE. Morning.

The member of staff has gone. BRUNO *relaxes and resumes putting books back on the shelves.*

What are you doing? Are the teaching staff here expected to do their own shelving?

BRUNO (*in hushed tones*). While my contemporaries have been fighting fascism on the Western Front, I have been tirelessly combating the fascists that run this library. The librarians are unforgiving and the fines, George, are, just beyond belief. So what I do is this: I conceal my overdue books in my bag, then sneak them in and place them back on the shelves. Then when I get another overdue notice, I storm in and say 'But I returned these books months ago.' They do a shelf check – and lo, there the books are – I get my fines written off and even an apology. Which I begrudgingly accept – most of the time. I save around two pounds a year.

GEORGE. Why don't you just return the books on time?

BRUNO. Where's the fun in that?

GEORGE. How much of that is true?

BRUNO. Good stories don't need to be true. You look crestfallen, George.

GEORGE. You're just not what I expected.

BRUNO. How? Did you think I would be taller?

GEORGE. No. Didn't you imagine more for yourself than this?

BRUNO. What a question to ask. I love this country. But it's an unrequited love. What can I do? I'm unwanted, but to leave is unimaginable. So here I am. Stuck on the outside. There are worse things. The world is made up of people who never quite get into the first team, who just miss the prizes at the flower show, who find themselves just drifting.

GEORGE. What if I made you an offer, to bring you right back to the heart of it all? I'd need you to sign the Official Secrets Act before we talk any more. I don't want to lie to you, Bruno. It's not easy work.

BRUNO. Not something to discuss with the wife and children then.

GEORGE. Not a problem for me.

BRUNO. Unmarried?

GEORGE. I still live with my old roommate from Oxford.

BRUNO. Oxford?! It gets worse. Thank you for thinking of me, George.

GEORGE. It was great to put a face to the name.

BRUNO. I'm teaching until October. If I said yes, when would I be needed?

GEORGE. Um, well, it's 10:30 now.

BRUNO. Right.

GEORGE. How would teatime sound to you?

BRUNO. Perfect. Actually.

GEORGE. You'll come then?

BRUNO. George –

GEORGE. Yes, Bruno?

BRUNO. I'll be on the next train to London.

AVA. Train ticket to London.

BRUNO *and* GEORGE *vanish, leaving* AVA *alone, back in the small room.*

JAMIE (*from offstage*). Coffee is ready!

VII

The Bronowski house. The kitchen

JAMIE *is slowly pushing down a cafetière plunger.* AVA *sits opposite him.*

JAMIE. This feels a bit like one of those coffee adverts. One-night stand. The man makes the woman a smooth coffee. She says –

AVA. Um – what great coffee. You have marvellous taste… Commander.

JAMIE. Commander?

AVA. Yeah, Commander.

JAMIE. Enjoy your luxury coffee. Tomorrow we slaughter the village. Would you like a bit of toast?

AVA. Okay. I want to ask you something –

JAMIE. I think I know what you're going to say.

AVA. Really?

JAMIE. And, yes, I would really like to see you again too.

AVA. Right.

JAMIE. That's not what you were going to say, was it?

AVA. I was going to ask if I could go through your family papers, in a professional capacity.

JAMIE. Right! No, that's not what I was expecting. Wow, this is embarrassing.

AVA. No, not at all. That's really nice of you to say.

JAMIE. Nice?

AVA. I'm sorry – I was given my notice at my job this afternoon.

JAMIE. Shit.

AVA. I've got so much on my mind. So this just wasn't what I – In just two weeks I'll be giving my last lecture.

JAMIE.... Shit. Sorry, I'm never good with knowing what to say.

AVA. And what do I do then? Apparently they're being very generous. The university keep using that word anyway: 'generous'. And I was just thinking this is an amazing, fortuitous, opportunity. Here's me, needing some new research. Something meaty to publish. And tonight, here's this huge archive. Of such a public figure. It could be a paper. It could even be another book.

JAMIE. You were pretty disparaging about him earlier.

AVA. No! Well, yes. Not about him. Just the way he sees things. I think he's wrong.

JAMIE. How is he wrong?

AVA. Your grandfather sees us moving in a straight line of progress. No wrong turns. No missteps. The *ascent* of man? Look, here, he said, I won't try and do the voice: 'The ascent of man is always teetering in the balance.'

BRUNO (*voice-over*). As we journey from advancement to advancement. There's always a sense of uncertainty that, when man lifts his foot for the next step, that we will come down ahead. But we always do.'

AVA. You agree with that?

JAMIE. We seem to be doing pretty well.

AVA. This is where it all started to go wrong.

JAMIE. The toast? Is it burnt?

AVA. No, wheat, farming. History's biggest fraud.

JAMIE. I think we need farming.

AVA. Why? Before we went where we wanted, when we wanted. But then we started farming wheat, we had to settle down, live permanently by the fields, completely changing our way of life –

JAMIE. Settling down isn't such a bad thing.

AVA. You know what it gave us?

JAMIE. Food?

AVA. We had food before. And more varied food! No. Fear. For the first time, fear about the future became a major player in the theatre of the human mind. What about the harvest next year? Or the year after that? We stopped living now. Wheat is why I'm terrified about losing my job, why your grandfather was so worried about whatever he was hiding in the room. It tied us down, and it made us afraid.

JAMIE. I knew there was a reason I've never liked granary bread. I feel vindicated.

AVA. But seriously – does that sound like progress to you? Of course it doesn't.

JAMIE. You never gave me an answer, by the way.

AVA. You never gave me an answer.

JAMIE. I don't know what's in that room. My grandmother – after Bruno died, I don't know if even my grandmother went through it.

High on the bookshelves, RITA *sits, watching* BRUNO*'s old documentaries.*

AVA. Even from a cursory look, I know your grandfather signed the Official Secrets Act. And look at this – '1944, July, first day at war offices. Whitehall.'

VIII

George and Bruno's wartime offices. 1944

As JAMIE *and* AVA *begin to dig through* BRUNO*'s locked room,* BRUNO *and* GEORGE *meet in their wartime offices for the first time.*

GEORGE. Bruno, you found us.

BRUNO. So is the mystery finally to be solved? Tell me, George, what will we be putting our minds to?

GEORGE. I'm so looking forward to collaborating. Here. But these instructions can't leave these rooms.

GEORGE *passes* BRUNO *a sealed envelope. He watches nervously as* BRUNO *opens it and reads.*

JAMIE. So? What were they working on?

AVA. It's not clear. These are his appointment diaries.

AVA *passes* JAMIE *a set of small diaries.* BRUNO *finishes reading his briefing. He is deep in thought.*

BRUNO. Right.

GEORGE. I warned you.

BRUNO. I hadn't expected this.

GEORGE. It's not too late to say no.

BRUNO. I'm… I'm thinking.

AVA *connects* BRUNO*'s thinking with the papers she's reading. Back as a lecturer, she addresses the audience.*

AVA. It's clearly something he's nervous about. Since humans first started working together, contradictions and conflict have been an inseparable part of every culture –

GEORGE (*to* BRUNO). I should say, it also gave me pause.

AVA. – our messy thoughts, feelings, desires and guilt compel us to think, criticise and change the world around us –

GEORGE. My parents are mathematicians. They've never had to – What a time to be alive. When you read mathematics, nobody prepares you for this.

AVA. – Consistency – well –

BRUNO. There are three questions to my mind. Should we do this? Well, maths itself, science itself, cannot be good or evil. It is either correct or incorrect, regardless of any later applications. Must we do this? The alternative is unimaginable. And can we do this?

AVA. – consistency is the playground of dull, inactive minds.

BRUNO. There was only one way to find out.

BRUNO strides to a large blackboard on the wall.

GEORGE. Right? Are we doing this?

BRUNO. It'd have to be a combination of geometry, topology, physics and – Are you with me, George?

BRUNO has noticed GEORGE is still uncertain.

GEORGE. Yes. I'm with you, Bruno.

We see GEORGE and BRUNO work together over the course of several months.

JAMIE. July 4. London. Slow day today with little progress. July 16 – still no progress, let alone a breakthrough. Wondering if the calculations we're attempting to correlate are even possible.

AVA. There are other sealed boxes. Shall I?

AVA retrieves more boxes from BRUNO's locked room.

JAMIE. July 24 –

BRUNO (*voice-over*). I have stared at the wall in my office so long I feel I could replicate every brick, crack and chip completely from memory. July 28 – still no significant progress. August 1 – No progress. August 8 – No progress.

More time passes. We hear and see extracts from the source books they are working through.

GEORGE (*voice-over*). Progress report to HQ. Week five. We are confident there is no way to work this out within the bounds of current mathematics.

TEXTBOOK (*voice-over*). This is because each point of X is open and so if X is infinite then the open cover consisting of the set of single points has no finite subcover.

GEORGE (*voice-over*). The decomposition theorem for finitely generated abelian groups states: If G is a finitely generated abelian group then G is isomorphic to –

BRUNO (*voice-over*). It's finding compatibility between geometry and physics in three dimensions. Time, speed, height, distance, altitude –

GEORGE (*voice-over*). If we use R, C, Z, N, Q to denote the set of real numbers, complex numbers, integers, natural numbers (or positive integers) and rational numbers respectively.

JAMIE *finds a small handwritten note that gets him excited.*

JAMIE. Look at this!

AVA. These are just small notes. Unrelated to work.

JAMIE. September 1. Spent most of the morning in an air-raid shelter.

Air-raid siren.

Air-raid shelter

GEORGE *and* BRUNO *sit in a shelter, deep underground.* GEORGE *writing a letter*, BRUNO *sits working.* JAMIE *is reading notes,* AVA *lives between both scenes. She finds a piece of paper in the diary.*

BRUNO. How much longer is this going to go on for?

GEORGE. This is the longest letter home I've ever written.

BRUNO. Are you boasting about our lack of progress?

GEORGE. No, Martyn and I – my housemate and I – went back to visit Oxford last week. Telling them about that. Promising them I'm still going to regular confession.

BRUNO. And are you?

GEORGE. Of course.

A distant bomb goes off.

JAMIE. Whatever he's doing: it's clearly some really high-level stuff though.

AVA. A lot of this is co-written. It's hard to see what direct input he had.

JAMIE. Come on! It's incredibly impressive. You can admit you were wrong.

GEORGE. That's the all-clear.

BRUNO. George – we're almost there.

George and Bruno's wartime offices

Work has picked up pace.

GEORGE. To HQ. Progress imminent. STOP. Feel solution to problems now only days away. STOP. Will report the moment breakthrough occurs. STOP.

BRUNO. I'm not going to sleep tonight. This will be racing through my mind.

GEORGE. Goodnight, Bruno.

BRUNO. Until tomorrow, George!

BRUNO *puts on his jacket and leaves the office.* RITA *enters, still in her black dress, and sits between* AVA *and* JAMIE.

AVA. Do you really think your grandmother – your family – never went through all this?

JAMIE. I don't know. What's that?

AVA. It's a newspaper clipping. A photograph of a young man, crying over his suitcase.

JAMIE. He looks like his whole world has ended. He's grieving, isn't he?

AVA. He looks like he's lost everything.

JAMIE. I know how he feels. To be the last one left.

AVA. Who is he?

JAMIE. I don't know. I've never seen it before.

RITA. And suddenly I remember who he reminded me of.

AVA. There are four more boxes in the room. Come, help me?

JAMIE. With pleasure!

RITA. His name, it was George. A boy who worked with my
husband. One morning, he just arrived at the house.

A large bomb goes off. GEORGE *appears at the house,
clearly shaken, his clothes covered in dust and dirt.*

GEORGE. Hello? Bruno? Are you here?

BRUNO *enters in from another room. Surprised to find*
GEORGE *at his home.*

BRUNO. George?

RITA*, remembering these events, slowly brings herself to be
a part of them again.*

RITA. Please, come and sit down.

BRUNO. Let me get you a strong drink.

BRUNO *exits. Silence.*

GEORGE. It's been eight hours.

RITA. I do remember now.

GEORGE. I'm still shaking. I was two streets away, walking
home from work. And as soon as I heard it, I knew. It's all
gone.

RITA. Eight hours? Where have you been?

GEORGE. Just there. Waiting.

RITA. Waiting for what?

GEORGE. Martyn. I live with a friend from Oxford called
Martyn. I was waiting for him to come home. His shift
pattern is always changing. So I didn't know whether he –

A long silence.

RITA. And did he come home?

Silence.

George. I'm so sorry.

GEORGE *takes a small, well-worn photograph out of his pocket and hands it to* RITA.

GEORGE. This is him.

RITA. There he is. You managed to salvage this?

GEORGE. No, I always have that on me. And because of what we do –

RITA. What you do?

GEORGE. What Bruno and I are working on.

RITA. He's not told me. We've never talked about it.

GEORGE. You should know.

RITA. He'll be back in a moment, let's –

GEORGE. You deserve to know.

RITA. I –

GEORGE. It's been hot this week.

Pause.

RITA. Yes, hasn't it?

GEORGE. At our final ball in Oxford, the weather was so hot, you could feel the sweat drip down your back. After years of pressure, to be free of all work and responsibility and drunk, was the best feeling in the world. It seemed to stay light forever, I walked back to my rooms in the early hours. At one in the morning the stone path was still hot. I was barefoot, I'd had my feet in the river. I smelt of sweat and tadpoles. I opened the window, threw off my shirt and felt the smallest breeze against my skin. I went into the bathroom to get some cold water, my head swaying and there he was, standing by the basin.

A sudden silence.

RITA. George – ?

GEORGE. I just froze. I saw him tense, just for a second,
sensing I was there. The hot air suddenly holding its breath.
He turned to face me. He was exactly as I knew he would be.
That's how I'll remember him. Totally unblemished. But
these invisible threads, they just held me back. I realise now
I have so many regrets.

RITA. You can't live a life full of regret, George.

GEORGE. I think I can. But I fear that I'm going to be alive for
a very, very long time. I killed him, you see.

RITA. You can't blame yourself.

GEORGE. Can't. Can't. Can't. I killed him a thousand times.
And every night, I kill him a thousand more.

  BRUNO *returns with a bottle, pouring* GEORGE *a drink.*

BRUNO. Here. Drink this. Are you up to working today?

RITA. Bruno –

There is a silence.

BRUNO. George, let's get this finished.

RITA. That was the first time I had any doubt in my husband.
I never told Bruno what George said to me. And I never saw
George again.

  BRUNO *and* GEORGE *return to their office.* BRUNO *shows*
  GEORGE *the completed mathematical proofs.*

BRUNO. This is it.

GEORGE. There it is.

BRUNO. Bringing everything we've done together.

GEORGE. You've done it. Well done, Bruno.

AVA. This is it.

JAMIE. What? You've worked it out, haven't you?

BRUNO. We've worked it out.

GEORGE. The final theory of fire-raising –

AVA. Fire-raising, Jamie.

BRUNO. Using small incendiary bombs.

AVA. They're calculating how to cause the most damage when dropping bombs.

JAMIE. Okay.

AVA. On civilian towns, and cities. On civilian women, on children –

High on the wall we look down on a GERMAN CIVILIAN *walking through a street in a foreign city.*

BRUNO. Using formulae for seven tonnes of aerial bombs.

A bomb in the distance falls, the GERMAN CIVILIAN *looks up, and keeps walking.*

Correctly deployed per square mile, using our calculation, they will result in more than two thousand civilians seriously injured.

A second bomb drops, this time closer. The GERMAN CIVILIAN *looks up again. And continues walking.*

AVA. We watch them now from the perspective of gods.

BRUNO. And more than fifteen thousand –

BRUNO/GEORGE. – civilians dead.

A third bomb drops, this time directly on top of the GERMAN CIVILIAN. *Who is pushed clear in the blast, as parts of the war room explode and papers fall to the floor.*

IX

In the stunned aftermath, GEORGE *and* BRUNO *tidy their office, packing away.*

GEORGE. It's always dying for your country, isn't it?

BRUNO. What is?

GEORGE. The honourable thing. Dying for your country. But nobody ever talks about killing for it.

JAMIE. This can't be right.

AVA. His handwritten notes are all over the papers.

JAMIE. Yes, but that doesn't prove anything. I don't believe he did this. I can't believe he would –

AVA. Jamie –

JAMIE. You don't know him like I do – he –

AVA. You never met him.

JAMIE. I feel like I –

BRUNO. Every bomb that we've helped fall, I've imagined my sweetheart standing beneath. And ask: was it this worth it?

GEORGE. And?

JAMIE. I feel like I know him.

AVA. Millions of people thought they knew him.

GEORGE. As a Christian, how could I have done this?

JAMIE. But he's my family.

BRUNO. As a Jew: how could I not?

JAMIE. He's all I've got left.

GEORGE. All this work and for what? To try and break the spirit of tens of thousands of women and children –

AVA (*speaks to the audience*). But their will was never going to break. The shared myths we create, the ideals we believe in, they may not be real but nothing is stronger. No earthquake can shake them, no ocean can drown them and no bomb can shatter the invisible threads that make our world. It doesn't stop us from trying, though.

JAMIE. I just *can't* believe it.

GEORGE. I could never go back now, to mathematics, it's betrayed me.

BRUNO. I don't know how I could go back either, but you're wrong, George.

GEORGE (*with huge sincerity*). Please, tell me how I'm wrong.

BRUNO. If anything, we have betrayed it. I shall miss working with you, George.

JAMIE. This changes everything. My grandfather... Tens of thousands of – I'm so sorry.

AVA. There's no need to apologise.

JAMIE. There's got to be something here that explains it. Let's go back into the room.

AVA. Jamie –

JAMIE. We've got to keep looking.

The radio on the table crackles on.

RADIO (*voice-over*). This is the BBC. Tonight we are reporting that the Allies air-bombing of Dresden has now resulted in forty thousand civilians dead. (*Static.*)

Last night in Nordhausen, in hours, Allied aircraft bombing has eliminated twenty per cent of their entire population. (*Static.*)

Throughout the course of the war, Berlin was the target of three hundred and sixty-three Allied bombing campaigns, killing tens of thousands and resulting in one-point-five million people homeless or sleeping on the street. (*Static.*)

A total of around six hundred thousand German civilians killed throughout the Second World War.

A huge tally on the blackboard shows the number of dead. AVA speaks to the audience.

AVA. The most surprising thing about Homo sapiens is that we
    are alone. There are no other species of human. Once there
    were: five, maybe six, maybe more. What became of them?
    There are the mass graves of Neanderthals, the bones of men
    and children, buried all across the world. Violence, justified,
    unjustified, is our most pronounced vestigial trait. You see,
    it's almost certain that our great-grandparents murdered
    every other variant of human species. Those invisible myths
    every other culture has, they mean so much to us, it's worth
    risking our very existence to protect what is, really, just
    emptiness in the air.

3.

X

BBC Radio recording booth

BRUNO. And the light will come on when I need to speak?

RADIO PRODUCER. Yes, when the light goes red, Dr Bronowski – we're broadcasting live.

BRUNO. Please call me Bruno. Everybody does.

RADIO PRODUCER. If you can just speak for the level check.

BRUNO. Of course. Um... Sorry, this is my first time on the radio.

RADIO PRODUCER. No problem. Why not tell me what you did during the war?

BRUNO. Well – actually I'm not allowed to talk about most of it.

RADIO PRODUCER. What did you do before the war then?

BRUNO. I worked in mathematics. At Cambridge, then at University of Hull. I don't do that now. I couldn't go back. Now, I have a desk job at the coal board. Nothing much to speak of. I'm – I'm just treading water.

RADIO PRODUCER. That's everything we need. When the light's on we're live. Just start talking.

BRUNO. How many people will be listening?

RADIO PRODUCER. Around fifteen million.

BRUNO. Only! Right. After the war, on a fine November day in 1945, I landed on an airstrip in Southern Japan, having been chosen as part of special task force. We had a week to research a commissioned report on how well the buildings had withstood the dropping of the nuclear bombs.

We drove off; night fell; the road rose and fell away, barren fields on all sides. Then, suddenly, I was aware that we were already at the centre of the damage.

The shadows behind me were not trees but the skeletons of the Mitsubishi factory buildings, pushed backwards and sideways as if by a giant hand of God.

BRUNO*'s voice shifts and* RITA *is now listening to it on the radio.*

But it was not God's hand. What I had thought to be broken rocks was a concrete powerhouse with its roof punched in. I could now make out the outline of two crumpled gasometers; otherwise there was nothing but cockeyed telegraph poles and loops of wire in a bare waste of ashes.

BRUNO *speaks live again.*

Elsewhere, the world was coming together again.

But how could anyone seeing this wasteland comprehend why this had been done? It had been justified. But in hindsight seemed unjustifiable.

Slow BRUNO*'s voice fades into the headphones of* JAMIE *and* AVA, *who are falling asleep. Listening together.*

Now, in the daylight of peacetime, who would understand what we had done? Perhaps not even our own families. The world would look at us as differently, like a son looks at his father differently on discovering he had shot and killed even a single man while away at war.

BRUNO *is back speaking again.*

We need to forcibly forget what we've done, who we are, lock it away, and, instead, imagine who we could become. Otherwise there's no hope for the future.

PRODUCER. And we're off the air.

Pause.

Dr Bronowski – Bruno –

BRUNO. How was it?

PRODUCER. You have really never done this before?

BRUNO. No, never.

PRODUCER. Have you ever considered doing more broadcast
work? I am producer of a show called –

XI

The Bronowski kitchen

RITA *is listening to the radio.* BRUNO *is in the studio of*
The Brains Trust. JAMIE *and* AVA *drink coffee, while* JAMIE
goes through the boxes.

BRAINS TRUST PRESENTER (*voice-over*). Welcome to
The Brains Trust. Where the public ask the nation's greatest
minds their most difficult questions.

Our guests tonight: novelist journalist and biographer,
Marghanita Laski, philosopher and broadcaster Bertrand
Russell, the first woman magistrate Sara Margery Fry, author
and theologist C. S. Lewis and, appearing for the very first
time on the panel, mathematician Dr Jacob Bronowski,
well-known to listeners for his Hiroshima Talk.

Now our first question is from Neil in Cambridge: 'With all
the war, death and destruction we have now endured, have
we lost our humanity?'

GEORGE *stands up and leaves.*

Why don't we start with you, Dr Bronowski?

BRUNO (*voice-over*). Ha. A gentle start. Thank you. 'Neil from
Cambridge.' What a big question. Well – yes – um – let me
see –

JAMIE *turns the radio off. Gets up and walks away.* AVA
follows after him.

RITA. I remember listening to that as if it were yesterday. And
you spending half an hour to decide what jacket to wear, to
go on the radio.

BRUNO. And what a disaster it was! I was humiliated.

RITA. Humiliated? Not at all!

BRUNO. That first pause. I must have been silent for minutes. Did you know, one of the key signals that British society has become extinct in a nuclear blast is BBC Radio stops broadcasting. And I gave them what felt like half an hour, forty minutes, fifty minutes of dead air! While I pondered, civilisation ceased to exist.

RITA. The broadcast was only twenty-five minutes long.

BRUNO. I was out of my depth.

RITA. The pause is the best part. When you hesitate – you're searching for the single word, out of the millions of possibilities, that will express precisely, exactly what you need it to. And it's so considered. As if all human development, the evolution and sophistication of language, has ripened to this moment where we can finally understand. In those moments, we are on the edge of our seats. Even I, who has listened to you for the vast majority of my lifetime.

BRUNO. Rita. (*Holds her hand for a moment in gratitude.*) You make it sound like it was such a chore.

RITA. Well, I used to only have to listen to you in the house. But then, I switch on the radio – there you are. I open the newspaper – there's an article you've written. Then the television. The only place I go for escape is the arts club.

BRUNO. I remember after that first *Brains Trust* rehearsing with you in the house.

RITA. Me asking you impossible questions all day long.

BRUNO. 'Ask me anything' –

RITA. Dr Bronowski –

BRUNO. Fire away!

RITA. Are there any secrets about you that I don't know?

BRUNO. Rita –

RITA. You don't need to answer.

BRUNO. Is this you asking? Or the interviewer? Because if it's you asking, I will tell you. You could find out –

RITA. I'm not asking you to tell me.

BRUNO. Well, then it's probably a little niche for the programme.

RITA. I don't want to know. I'm sure. I've already lost you once. I don't want to risk finding that I never really knew you at all.

BRUNO. You knew me, Rita.

RITA. But it's time to say goodbye, Bruno.

BRUNO. Goodbye?

RITA. When you first were gone, I used to indulge myself, imagining talking with you like this. Imagining playing and sparring with you. But as this doubt crept in, I did it more and more. Until this house was full of ghosts. I'll never be certain, and I'm happy with that now. But I need to get on with life. I'll see you, when I see you.

BRUNO. Rita, you were the best person I knew.

RITA. I always suspected that.

BRUNO. And considering most of this conversation is taking place in your own mind, potentially, you're also the most arrogant.

RITA. I'll live with that.

BRUNO. Before I go, I have something to ask you.

RITA. My audition for *The Brains Trust* now, is it?

BRUNO. Indeed. Rita Bronowski – tell me, what was it like being in love?

RITA. Well, when I first met my husband – Bruno, I think his name was, is – I drew him. I think that's the perfect analogy for falling in love. When you first fall in love, you're besotted with the image of them you've sketched in your mind. When the pencil sketch fades, you'll see them for who they truly are.

But, if you can fall in love with them that second time, embracing all that tentative uncertainty, well, it's the only thing worth living for. And now… forty more years.

RITA *exits*.

XII

AVA. I really should get going. It's almost dawn.

JAMIE. I'm sorry, I've been – I just didn't know. I'm glad that app doesn't have a rating option. Nobody would ever meet me again.

AVA. It's alright to be shocked. I don't think anybody knows. That's what makes it so –

JAMIE. Awful.

AVA. Exciting. Awful and exciting. It shows a different side of your grandfather. None of us are prepared to make any of these decisions. Your grandfather was faced with his whole race and religion being exterminated.

JAMIE. Sorry for freaking out. And thank you for understanding. I'm glad it was you I met. I know I can trust you. I know you'll keep this just between us. You're not the sort of person, now you know what we're dealing with, who's going to run off and write articles about this. Or stand up and tell all your students. You're not like that. I already can't wait to see you again.

AVA. Jamie, I don't want to see you again. I just wanted this. Not even this really.

JAMIE. Why didn't you say something –

AVA. I thought I was clear. And I didn't want to –

JAMIE. Miss the chance to go through all my family papers? Get the dirt on my grandfather? Christ.

AVA. Jamie – I didn't plan any of this.

JAMIE. Yeah, but there must have been a moment though. Where you knew what I wanted, and what you wanted, and you didn't say anything.

AVA. What you want, Jamie, none of that stuff really exists. I'm in a corner, Jamie. I could lose everything. That's real.

JAMIE. You'll ruin his reputation. My family's reputation.

AVA. You will be fine, Jamie. I don't live in a big house like this. I'm the one about to lose my job, my career, everything. I'll do whatever I need to do. I can't – I won't – make you any promises.

JAMIE. I thought you were better than that.

AVA. You didn't know him and you don't know me. I'll see myself out. I'm only human, Jamie.

JAMIE. Whatever 'human' means.

4.

XIII

AVA *turns to talk to us. Once again out of time, leaving* JAMIE *alone in the kitchen.*

AVA. And we're finally here. At the big question. The question –

AVA/BRUNO. – I have dedicated my whole career/life to answering.

BRUNO. Human is something we have all become. First, across millions of years. And then each of us, across our own lifetimes. In both cases, it's not immediate. To become human is a gradual, beautiful evolution.

AVA. To be human is to be hurt. Is to be destructive and damaging. And selfish, only really looking out for ourselves. To be human is to do everything you need to survive.

BRUNO. Well, whatever it means to be human, we seem to have fallen out of love with it.

AVA. There's something we finally agree on.

JAMIE *exits.*

BRUNO. What are you going to do?

AVA *makes her way through the house to* BRUNO's *locked room.*

AVA. I'm going to publish. I was always going to publish.

BRUNO. It must be tempting and easy to close your eyes to history and speculate that everything undesirable – greed, violence, our selfishness – are primal animal instincts. Always with us. But you're wrong.

AVA *is taking boxes and papers off the shelves, at a fast pace.*

AVA. You're not going to convince me otherwise.

BRUNO. As if, like a tiger, we still have to kill to survive.
  We don't.

AVA. Say what you like.

BRUNO. I always have.

AVA. I asked you before, how can you, of all people, Bruno,
  seem so sure.

BRUNO. 'Of all people'? I did start out so sure. Of so much.

AVA. But now?

BRUNO. When we look at the carvings of the early gods now,
  we are looking at ourselves. We are healers of the sick, masters
  over nature, we're the ones who rain terror and fire rain from
  the sky. Who can destroy every last human, if we wish.

  I was at Nagasaki, we filmed at Auschwitz for *Ascent of Man*.

  AVA *has slowed and now they are fully engaged.*

AVA. Bruno –

BRUNO. Wait. I was there. At the two mass graveyards of the
  twentieth century. I stood above a small pool of water, where
  tens of millions of people, my own family were flushed,
  I saw what we are capable of. It was not done by gas. By
  mathematics. It was done by dogma. When we think we have
  absolute knowledge, with no test in reality, this is how we
  behave. When we close our eyes and our ears, we stop being
  human. We become just regiments of ghosts. Everything
  I have done, the pursuit of science, of knowledge, has been
  a tribute to what we can know although we are fallible.

AVA. Yet you say we always come down ahead.

BRUNO. Because we have. We have come close to succumbing.
  The problem with the world is that fanatics are always so sure.
  And wiser people, those who question, are consumed by
  doubt. I wanted to be sure in my uncertainty. Confident that
  I knew nothing. That is how I, of all people, have hope.

AVA. 'The only thing we've learned from history –

AVA/BRUNO. – is that we don't learn from history.'

BRUNO. I finished that broadcast, standing above that small pool of water, by saying: 'In the words of Oliver Cromwell "I beseech you, in the bowels of Christ, think it possible you may be mistaken".'

XIV

The Bronowski house. 1973

The darkened hall. In the next room a party is in full swing.

GEORGE. Bruno?

BRUNO. George. Hello!

GEORGE. I hope I'm not intruding.

BRUNO. Of course not. I've not heard from you in years.

GEORGE. Life has got in the way.

BRUNO. You don't look a day older.

GEORGE. I look considerably older.

BRUNO. That is what I meant.

GEORGE. Being a father of twins does that to you.

BRUNO. Congratulations.

GEORGE. Sorry I've been out of touch. I was just passing and thought I'd – But you're clearly having a party.

BRUNO. It's just some friends – I've just finished filming a television series.

GEORGE. I listen to you on the radio, sometimes.

BRUNO. Really?

GEORGE. I like to hear you. You always sound so confident.

BRUNO. Thank you.

GEORGE. You always did. I think about our work most days.
I wanted to show you something. I've cut it out of the paper.

BRUNO. What is it?

GEORGE. It's a young German solider, who's returned home to
find his house and family gone.

There is a pause while BRUNO *examines the photo.*

I can't stop thinking about it. Seeing it. Keep it. Please. Is
there anything you can say about it?

BRUNO. Sometimes there are no words.

GEORGE. I look forward to your series.

BRUNO. *The Ascent of Man.*

GEORGE. I'll watch out for it.

BRUNO. The final episode was actually filmed here. (*Fades
into presenting.*) Everything has taught me that man's life,
a man's home, is the proper place to study our biological
uniqueness. It is where man can truly be him or herself. It is
where our children, the future, are brought up and moulded.
And it is where all our secrets are kept.

AVA *has appeared, where* GEORGE *left. She catches*
BRUNO*'s eye.*

Secrets no more...

BRUNO *holds up his wine glass to make a speech to his
guests, clinking it with a fork.*

Thank you all for coming. At the beginning, I did not know
if I could make this series. I did not know if I had it in me to
see it through. We are all afraid. Even here. For ourselves,
for our families, for the future. That is the nature of the
human imagination.

Knowledge is the unending adventure on the edge of
uncertainty.

And every time I step out in front of the camera to talk to
you all, I am afraid. Yet, every man, every civilisation, has
gone forward because of its engagement of what it has set

out to do. The personal commitment of a person to their skill. The emotional, physical and intellectual, working as one has made the ascent of man.

He lowers his glass. BRUNO *is now with us in the room, talking directly to the audience.*

Every animal leaves traces of what it was; humans alone leave traces of what they have created. And this series is what I will leave. To speak for me when I can no longer speak for myself.

He beckons to AVA. *Looking out at the audience. The house lights slightly raise.*

Just look at them, that great escape – no more generations of men wiped out at war, you are now more likely to be harmed by excess than from starvation or famine. Even the poorest amongst you has medical care Queen Victoria herself would have envied.

How could anyone say we are not coming down ahead? And perhaps, if you continue working together, we might only just be getting started?

AVA. What Bruno doesn't realise –

BRUNO. Yes?

AVA. Is that this will be his very last television interview.

XV

Backstage at *Parkinson*

BRUNO *is backstage at* Parkinson, *he is aware he is back near the end.*

PARKINSON PRODUCER. Dr Bronowksi, Mr Parkinson has arrived. We're setting up the studio.

BRUNO. Thank you.

RITA *enters, the first time we're seeing her not in mourning, in real time.*

RITA. Sorry I'm running late.

BRUNO. Rita, I didn't think you were going to make it.

RITA. Look at you. I can tell you're nervous.

BRUNO. Nervous? No. I feel a little tired.

RITA. What is he going to ask you that you can't answer?

BRUNO. You're right. I just feel, like I'm at the end of a very long task.

PARKINSON PRODUCER. Dr Bronowski –

BRUNO. Here we go.

PARKINSON. We're ready for you.

BRUNO. Call me Bruno. Everybody does.

BRUNO *steps off.*

PARKINSON (*video*). I'm often asked which is my favourite interview. One such occurred just over two years ago when I interviewed a remarkable man, Mr Jacob Bronowski. Sadly, eighteen months ago, Dr Bronowski died. I believe it to be the testament to a rare human being. I shall forever remember this meeting.

RITA *exits.*

XVIV

AVA. I realise I've run over. You must have other lectures to go to. But thank you for listening. I'm not when – or if – we will see each other again. But I hope we do. Wherever that may be.

RITA *enters with a reel-to-reel projector. It plays.*

BRAINS TRUST PRESENTER (*voice-over*). From Janet in Salisbury – if the panel could leave a piece of advice for our descendants, what would it be? Bertrand Russell – your answer.

AVA. Maybe, maybe I'm wrong. By the way. Maybe I was wrong.

BERTRAND RUSSSELL (*video*). In this world that is getting more and more closely interconnected, we have to learn to tolerate each other if we are to live together and not die together. We must learn a kind of charity and tolerance, which is absolutely vital to the continuation of human life on this planet.

As RITA *watches,* BRUNO *slowly enters.*

RITA. Bruno?

BRUNO. You took your time getting here.

RITA. I prefer to think of myself as fashionably late.

BRUNO. Did you miss me?

RITA. Of course not. I married fifty more times.

BRUNO. And yet you waited up for me.

AVA. So, how will it end? Somewhere, one day, it is – almost – inevitable there will be the very last set of human footprints.

Not knowing where we're going, we'll carry on journeying until the very things that keep us alive – our willingness to work together, our powerful, shared imaginations, our uncertainty – fall away. If we let them.

BRUNO. Rita, let me show you a future I know is possible, if our potential is fully realised. Let me show you what could come next.

We see two HUMAN FIGURES *walking alone.*

AVA. Therefore those final footprints will be from people, not holding hands, but walking alone. The tracks of our last descendants, after such a long journey, will be walking when, without warning, something causes them to stop –

RITA *and* BRUNO *turn.* BRUNO *covers* RITA*'s eyes.*

BRUNO. Ready?

RITA. As ready as I'll ever be. Bruno…

BRUNO. Rita. I know.

AVA. – and turn.

BRUNO. Everything we can imagine for the future –

AVA. And, for the last time.

BRUNO. – it's all possible. Just –

AVA/BRUNO. – look.

The two HUMAN FIGURES *turn and make eye contact with the audience. Blackout.*

End of Play.

www.nickhernbooks.co.uk

facebook.com/nickhernbooks

twitter.com/nickhernbooks